Glances of Japan

日本文化とおもてなし英語

坂部俊行／岡島徳昭／ Howard Tarnoff

NAN'UN-DO

Glances of Japan

Toshiyuki Sakabe / Noriaki Okajima / Howard Tarnoff

Download Audio

音声ファイル
無料 DL
のご案内

このテキストの音声を無料で視聴（ストリーミング）・ダウンロード
できます。自習用音声としてご活用ください。
以下のサイトにアクセスしてテキスト番号で検索してください。

https://nanun-do.com　テキスト番号［ **512020** ］

※ 無線 LAN（WiFi）に接続してのご利用を推奨いたします。

※ 音声ダウンロードは Zip ファイルでの提供になります。
お使いの機器によっては別途ソフトウェア（アプリケーション）
の導入が必要となります。

はじめに

2019年秋，縦横無尽に走る桜ジャージの活躍で，空前のラグビーブームを巻き起こした「ラグビーワールドカップ2019日本大会」，新型コロナウイルス感染拡大により開催延期を余儀なくされた一方で，世界が待ち望む「東京2020オリンピック・パラリンピック競技大会」，さらには2025年5月，55年ぶり開催予定の「2025年日本国際博覧会（大阪・関西万博）」と国際イベントが目白押しの日本。日本政府観光局統計訪日客数の推移をみると，12年前の2009年には年間700万人に届かなかった訪日客数が，2018年には3000万人を突破しました。

押し寄せるグローバル化の波。現代日本社会では，これまでにもまして，国際社会で主体的に活躍できる学生の育成が求められています。世界を舞台に活躍する国際人に近づくためには，語学力に加えて，自国の文化に対する関心を深めることも大切になります。

本テキストは，これらのことを念頭に，語学の学習を通し，自国の文化にも興味を抱いてもらえるよう配慮しています。全15章各章4ページの本書は，ワンセメスター用大学教材として使用できるよう構成されています。本教材を通して，語学のスキルを上達させると同時に，自国についても関心をもっていただけることを願います。

最後になりましたが，本書出版にあたり企画の段階から的確なアドバイスを頂きました南雲堂の原島亮氏，そして伊藤宏実氏に心から御礼申し上げます。

2019夏　著書一同

本書の使い方

インバウンド観光の現状を見ると，訪日外国人旅行者数は年々増加し，政府は 2020 年までに 4000 万人という目標を掲げています。また，文部科学省やその他省庁では，「グローバル戦略」を展開する一環として，2020 年を目途に留学生の受け入れ 30 万人を目指す「留学生 30 万人計画」策定しています。増加とともにニーズも多様化し，英語の必要性はどんどん高まるばかりです。

本書では，訪日外国人に関係するであろう 15 の場所・項目等を選択し，以下のように各ユニットを構成しています。

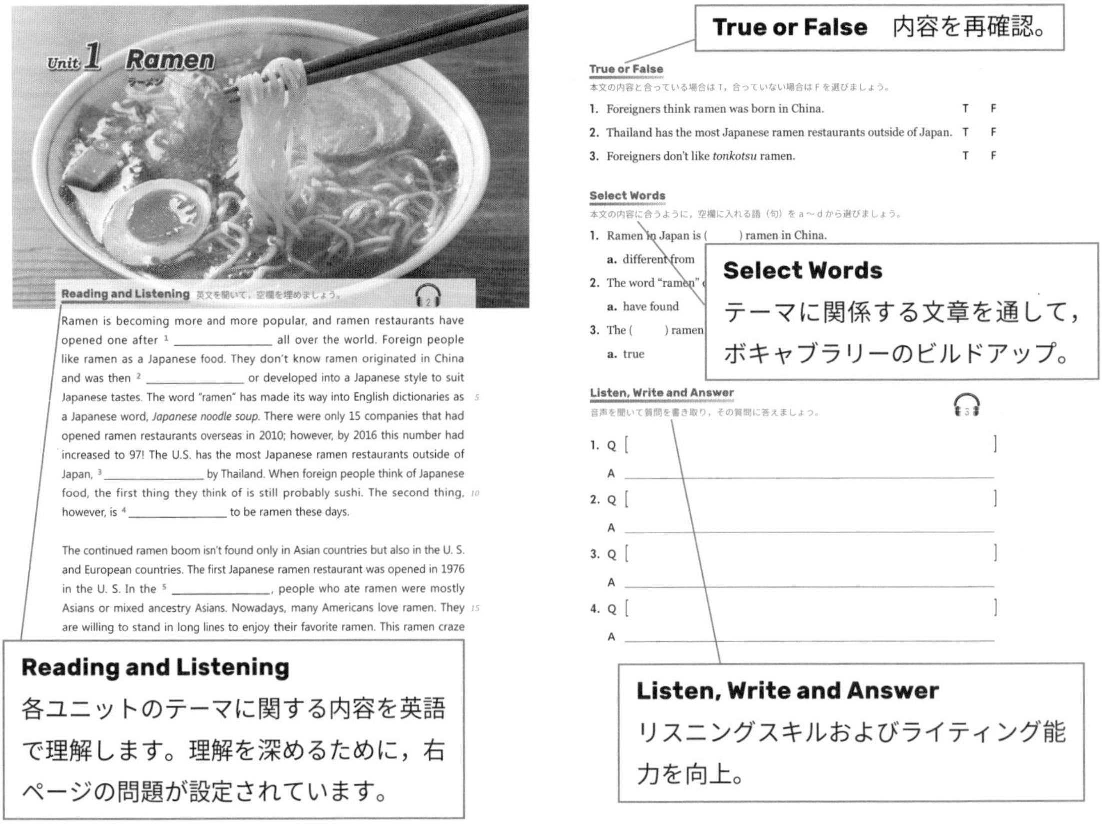

Conversation

様々なアルバイトの場面での，顧客との英語によるやり取りを練習します。各ユニットのテーマに関わる場所で，アルバイト学生（学習者）がそこに訪れる外国人留学生（Jack）を接客するという設定です。ユニットによっては，Jack が友人と一緒に訪れるという設定もあります。例文の会話を参考にし，会話の流れを考えながら，その後に続くセリフを各自で考えてペアワークをします。

Conversation 4

あなた（A）はラーメン店でアルバイトをしています。そこに外国人 Jack（B）が来店しました。食券の購入方法を説明する会話文の続きを作成し，パートナーとやり取りをしましょう。

At a ramen restaurant

A: いらっしゃいませ。Hello. How many in your party, sir?

B: Two.

A: I'm sorry, all our tables are taken right now. Are seats at the counter OK?

B: Sure.

A: I will get the seats ready for you. It will just be a few minutes.

B: OK.

A: お二人ご案内します！ Do you know how to order? You will first need to buy a ticket at the vending machine here.

Continue the Conversation

会話を続けましょう。

B:

A:

B:

A:

B:

A:

Useful Words and Phrases

insert : 入れる ⇒ Insert 500 yen.
press : 押す ⇒ Press this button.
Would you like ~ : ~いかがですか ⇒ Would you like a glass of water?
How do you like ~ : ~はいかがしますか ⇒ How do you like your noodles?
thick : 濃い・厚い ⇒ I like my soup thick.
thin : 薄い・細い ⇒ I like my soup thin.
flavor : 味 ⇒ Which flavor do you like?
Here is ~. / Here you are. : どうぞ・~です ⇒ Here is your ramen.
anything else : 他に何か ⇒ Would you like anything else?
accept : 受けつける・認める ⇒ We only accept cash. / We also accept most credit cards.

Useful Words and Phrases

各場面で使用できる語句や表現を紹介しています。

Message to a Friend 5

次の電子メールを読み，下記の質問に答えなさい。

Hi Saki,

I'm writing you to let you know that I ate real Sapporo ramen last night in Tokyo. I went with a good friend of mine, Ken. He studies English very hard so that he can

Message to a Friend

電子メールを通して，さらなる読解力そしてライティング能力を養います。全ユニットを通じて，日本の大学に留学している Jack が同じ大学に通う日本人の友達の Saki へ，日本で経験する様々な出来事や場面をシェアして，日本文化を理解していくという設定となっています。送信者と受信者が逆になっているユニットもあります。電子メールの後には，その内容に関わる設問があります。

4. What kind of ramen will he eat next week?

Write your reply to Jack 上記のメールへの返信を書いてみましょう。

さらにはそのメールへの返信を書いてみるというアクティビティがあります。

本書を通して，日本の文化や習慣を再確認・再認識し，それらを英語で理解して説明できるようにしましょう。また，様々なアルバイトの場面で，日本を訪れている外国人観光客へのおもてなしを習得しましょう。

Contents

Unit 1
Ramen 8

Unit 2
Animal Café 12

Unit 3
Stand-up Eatery 16

Unit 4
Convenience Store 20

Unit 5
Japanese Fast Food, Gyudon 24

Unit 6
Japanese Spa 28

Unit 7
Flour Dishes 32

Unit 8
Karaoke 36

Unit 9
Seating Charges at Japanese Restaurants 40

Unit 10
Second-Hand Store 44

Unit 11
Kawaii Culture 48

Unit 12
Soba 52

Unit 13
Bento 56

Unit 14
Shrine 60

Unit 15
Onsen 64

Unit 1 Ramen

ラーメン

Reading and Listening 英文を聞いて，空欄を埋めましょう。 2

Ramen is becoming more and more popular, and ramen restaurants have opened one after 1 ________________ all over the world. Foreign people like ramen as a Japanese food. They don't know ramen originated in China and was then 2 ________________ or developed into a Japanese style to suit Japanese tastes. The word "ramen" has made its way into English dictionaries as a Japanese word, *Japanese noodle soup*. There were only 15 companies that had opened ramen restaurants overseas in 2010; however, by 2016 this number had increased to 97! The U.S. has the most Japanese ramen restaurants outside of Japan, 3 ________________ by Thailand. When foreign people think of Japanese food, the first thing they think of is still probably sushi. The second thing, however, is 4 ________________ to be ramen these days.

The continued ramen boom isn't found only in Asian countries but also in the U.S. and European countries. The first Japanese ramen restaurant was opened in 1976 in the U.S. In the 5 ________________, people who ate ramen were mostly Asians or Asian Americans. Nowadays, many Americans love ramen. They are willing to stand in long lines to enjoy their favorite ramen. This ramen craze in the U.S. has 6 ________________ to European countries. The most popular flavor is *tonkotsu*.

(207 words)

True or False

本文の内容と合っている場合はＴ，合っていない場合はＦを選びましょう。

1. Foreigners think ramen was born in China. T F
2. Thailand has the most Japanese ramen restaurants outside of Japan. T F
3. Foreigners don't like *tonkotsu* ramen. T F

Select Words

本文の内容に合うように，空欄に入れる語（句）を a ～ d から選びましょう。

1. Ramen in Japan is (　　　) ramen in China.

   a. different from　**b.** the same as　**c.** better than　**d.** worse than

2. The word "ramen" can be (　　　) in an English dictionary.

   a. have found　**b.** found　**c.** finding　**d.** find

3. The (　　　) ramen of foreigners is *tonkotsu* flavor.

   a. true　**b.** always　**c.** favorite　**d.** almost

Listen, Write and Answer

音声を聞いて質問を書き取り，その質問に答えましょう。

3

1. Q [　　　　　　　　　　　　　　　　　　　　]

   A ____

2. Q [　　　　　　　　　　　　　　　　　　　　]

   A ____

3. Q [　　　　　　　　　　　　　　　　　　　　]

   A ____

4. Q [　　　　　　　　　　　　　　　　　　　　]

   A ____

Conversation

あなた（A）はラーメン店でアルバイトをしています。そこに外国人 Jack（B）が来店しました。食券の購入方法を説明する会話文の続きを作成し，パートナーとやり取りをしましょう。

At a ramen restaurant

A: いらっしゃいませ。Hello. How many in your party, sir?

B: Two.

A: I'm sorry, all our tables are taken right now. Are seats at the counter OK?

B: Sure.

A: I will get the seats ready for you. It will just be a few minutes.

B: OK.

A: お二人ご案内します！ Do you know how to order? You will first need to buy a ticket from the ticket machine at the entrance.

Continue the Conversation

会話を続けましょう。

B:

A:

B:

A:

B:

A:

Useful Words and Phrases

insert : ～を入れる ⇒ Insert 500 yen.
press : 押す ⇒ Press this button.
Would you like ~? : ～はいかがですか ⇒ Would you like a glass of water?
How do you like ~? : ～はいかがしますか ⇒ How do you like your noodles?
thick : 濃い，厚い ⇒ I like my soup thick.
thin : 薄い，細い ⇒ I like my soup thin.
flavor : 味 ⇒ Which flavor do you like?
Here is ~. / Here you are. : どうぞ・～です ⇒ Here is your ramen.
anything else : 他に何か ⇒ Would you like anything else?
accept : ～を受けつける，認める ⇒ We only accept cash. / We also accept most credit cards.

Message to a Friend

5

次の電子メールを読み，下記の質問に答えなさい。

Hi Saki,

I'm writing you to let you know that I ate real Sapporo ramen last night in Tokyo. I went with a good friend of mine, Ken. He studies English very hard so that he can study abroad in the future. He is crazy about ramen. He eats ramen three or four times a week! He took me to a very popular ramen restaurant called *Sumo Ramen*. The chef trained in one of Sapporo's most famous ramen restaurants. He then opened the restaurant in Tokyo last year. They buy their noodles from a noodle manufacturer in Sapporo. Their specialty is miso flavor, so I ordered miso ramen with a seasoned egg, *ajitama*. I also ordered a bowl of rice, which went really well with the ramen. The ramen restaurant also sells their own instant ramen. I bought a few packs, so I will give some to you. I'm sure you'll like them.

There are many ramen restaurants here. We can enjoy various local specialties without having to visit the local city. I will try *Iekei* ramen tomorrow and Hakata ramen next week. *Iekei* ramen originated in Yokohama and features a pork soy-sauce flavored soup with thick, straight noodles. I will write to you to let you know how it tastes.

Sincerely,
Jack

(213 words)

1. When did the ramen restaurant open?

---

2. What kind of ramen is *Sumo Ramen* famous for?

---

3. What did he order with his ramen?

---

4. What kind of ramen will he eat next week?

Write your reply to Jack

上記のメールへの返信を書いてみましょう。

Unit 2 Animal Café

アニマルカフェ

Reading and Listening 英文を聞いて，空欄を埋めましょう。

Many people go to a café to enjoy a cup of coffee, [1] ________________ meals or sweets. But there are some people who visit a particular café for a unique purpose. A good example of this is a *neko* café, or cat café. Cat lovers go there to enjoy [2] ________________ time and playing with cats. It is said that the first cat café opened in Taiwan in 1998. The first cat café in Japan is said to have opened in Osaka in 2004.

A cat café [3] ________________ the animal café boom in Japan. Nowadays, there aren't only cat cafés but also many kinds of animal cafés, such as owl cafés, rabbit cafés, snake cafés and even hedgehog cafés. People who live in a [4] ________________ society are often under a lot of stress. One way to reduce stress is to visit an animal café. You can enjoy a cup of coffee while being in contact with animals.

These days, animal cafés are a popular [5] ________________ for foreign tourists in Japan. Animal cafés have frequently been reported in the foreign media. Also, many foreign visitors in Japan have [6] ________________ about Japanese animal cafés on social media. Many animal cafés have opened in other countries.

(201 words)

True or False

本文の内容と合っている場合は T，合っていない場合は F を選びましょう。

1. The first cat café is said to have opened in Japan.　　T　　F
2. Foreign tourists in Japan like to visit animal cafés.　　T　　F
3. There are no animal cafés in foreign countries.　　T　　F

Select Words

本文の内容に合うように，空欄に入れる語（句）を a ～ d から選びましょう。

1. Animal cafés are (　　　) a place to reduce stress.

   a. run with　　**b.** familiar with　　**c.** known as　　**d.** spent as

2. People enjoy (　　　) cats at cat cafés.

   a. be touched　　**b.** touch　　**c.** touched　　**d.** touching

3. Animal cafés are one of the (　　　) places for foreign tourists to visit.

   a. unknown　　**b.** favorite　　**c.** dangerous　　**d.** disappointing

Listen, Write and Answer

音声を聞いて質問を書き取り，その質問に答えましょう。

7

1. Q [　　　　　　　　　　　　　　　　　　　　　　　　　　]

   A ____

2. Q [　　　　　　　　　　　　　　　　　　　　　　　　　　]

   A ____

3. Q [　　　　　　　　　　　　　　　　　　　　　　　　　　]

   A ____

4. Q [　　　　　　　　　　　　　　　　　　　　　　　　　　]

   A ____

Conversation

あなた（A）はネコカフェでアルバイトをしています。そこに外国人 Jack（B）が来店しました。初めてネコカフェ来たという設定で会話文の続きを作成し，パートナーとやり取りをしましょう。

At a cat café

A: Hello. Welcome to Cat Lovers' Paradise.

B: Hi. A table for two, please. My friend will join me later.

A: Do you prefer a table or a sofa?

B: Sofa, please.

A: This way, please.

B: Thank you.

A: Have you ever been to a cat café before?

Continue the Conversation

会話を続けましょう。

B:

A:

B:

A:

B:

A:

Useful Words and Phrases

all-you-can-drink : 飲み放題 ⇒ What is included in the all-you-can-drink course?
cream and sugar : ミルクと砂糖 ⇒ I'd like cream and sugar in my coffee.
sharing a table : 相席 ⇒ Would you mind sharing a table with other customers?
combo / meal set : セットメニュー ⇒ A hot dog combo with an iced tea please.
help yourself to : ～をご自由にどうぞ ⇒ Please help yourself to water.
come with : ～付 ⇒ All meals come with soup and a salad.
Today's special : 今日のおすすめ ⇒ Today's special is teriyaki chicken.
allergy/allergic : アレルギー（の）⇒ I'm allergic to cats.
with/without : ～付で / ～なしで ⇒ I want it with rice. / I want it without *wasabi*.
lint roller : コロコロ ⇒ Do you have a lint roller?

Message to a Friend

次の電子メールを読み，下記の質問に答えなさい。

Hi Saki,

Can you guess where my friend Satoru took me yesterday? We went to a *neko* café. He loves cats and has been to the café before. There were many cats walking around or taking a nap inside the café. We could touch, hold and play with them. They were very cute. When I was a kid, I had a dog named Elvis. I've never had cats before, but they are adorable. The café had many cat toys that we could use. I used a cat feather toy. I could play with a cat using that toy forever. It was really fun. Also, their food menu for customers was good. I ordered a chicken teriyaki special.

I met a couple of foreign visitors at the café. They were from Germany staying a few weeks in Japan. Visiting a *neko* café was one of their highlights during this trip. They saw a *neko* café on YouTube and wanted to visit. They said that they didn't have any *neko* cafés in Germany. They were talking about opening one in Germany.

Satoru and I are planning to go to a different animal café next week. I would also like to go to a snake café if there are any around.

Kind regards,
Jack

(211 words)

1. Where did Jack go with Satoru?

2. What was the name of Jack's dog?

3. Who did Jack meet at the café?

4. Where may Jack and Satoru go next week?

Write your reply to Jack

上記のメールへの返信を書いてみましょう。

Unit 3 Stand-up Eatery

立ち食い

Reading and Listening 英文を聞いて，空欄を埋めましょう。 10

Stand-up eating is one 1 ________________ of Japanese culture. Stand-up-eating establishments are perfect places for businesspeople who are busy and don't have enough time to sit and enjoy eating lunch.

The origin of stand-up-eating stalls dates back to the Edo period. In those days, there were many street 2 ________________ of soba, sushi and tempura. Soba was particularly popular because it was easy to prepare and eat with just the right texture. There have been stand-up-eating soba-noodle stands at numerous train stations all over Japan for a long time. People are lured by the 3 ________________ of soba noodles.

In recent years, stand-up fine dining has become popular. People can enjoy premium steak, exquisite French dishes, delicious Italian food and authentic Japanese food at inexpensive prices. 4 ________________ of the economic conditions, people have a desire to dine out. Stand-up fine dining requires a relatively small business space. The owner can save a good amount of money on rent and personnel cost, 5 ________________ them to offer quality dishes at lower prices. Their target customers are young businesspeople and women. Since the shop space is 6 ________________ and tables are arranged close to each other, stand-up dining is a good place to get to know other customers.

(201 words)

True or False

本文の内容と合っている場合はT，合っていない場合はFを選びましょう。

1. Stand-up dining first appeared in the Edo period. T F
2. People enjoy eating soba noodles only at train stations. T F
3. Stand-up fine dining places offer quality food with high prices. T F

Select Words

本文の内容に合うように，空欄に入れる語（句）をa～dから選びましょう。

1. Stand-up eating is one aspect of Japanese culture (　　　).
   a. without wonder　**b.** without doubt　**c.** with suspicion　**d.** with question
2. People are attracted (　　　) the smell of soba.
   a. to　**b.** with　**c.** of　**d.** for
3. Stand-up fine dining places offer food at (　　　) prices.
   a. high　**b.** unfair　**c.** reasonable　**d.** expensive

Listen, Write and Answer

音声を聞いて質問を書き取り，その質問に答えましょう。

11

1. Q [　　　　　　　　　　　　　　　　　　　　　　　　]
   A ____
2. Q [　　　　　　　　　　　　　　　　　　　　　　　　]
   A ____
3. Q [　　　　　　　　　　　　　　　　　　　　　　　　]
   A ____
4. Q [　　　　　　　　　　　　　　　　　　　　　　　　]
   A ____

Conversation

12

あなた（A）は立ち飲み屋でアルバイトをしています。その店で外国人 Jack（B）とその友人が食事をしています。会話文の続きを作成し，パートナーとやり取りをしましょう。

At a stand-up diner

A: May I help you?

B: Yes. May we have two extra plates?

A: Certainly. How's the food?

B: Delicious. When did you first open?

A: It's been two years now.

B: Is that so?

A: Would you like some dessert?

Continue the Conversation

会話を続けましょう。

B:

A:

B:

A:

B:

A:

Useful Words and Phrases

Do you mind ~? : ～してもいいですか ⇒ Do you mind if I join you?
share : 分ける ⇒ We'd like to share a salad.
on me : 私のおごり ⇒ The dinner is on me.
plate : 取り皿 ⇒ Can we have extra plates?
special : おすすめ ⇒ What is the special today?
specialty : 名物 ⇒ The specialty of the restaurant is steak.
doggie bag : 持ち帰り用容器（袋）⇒ Let's ask for a doggie bag.
side order : サイドメニュー ⇒ Would you like a side order of anything?
refill : おかわり ⇒ Could I have a refill of coffee?
check : 会計 ⇒ Check, please.

Message to a Friend

13

次の電子メールを読み，下記の質問に答えなさい。

Hi Saki,

The other day you mentioned a *tachinomi* dining spot you went to with friends from the university club you are a member of. As I remember, you belong to the Rakugo Society, *Ochiken*, right? I think you told me you would have a recital next month. Anyway, getting back to *tachinomi* dining, I went to one in Shibuya with an exchange student from Korea. We were able to try some delicious French food there without paying top prices. There were no chairs, so we had to stand while eating and drinking.

Each table was pretty small. But no one complained about it because of the quality of their food and the inexpensive prices. I was very satisfied with the sophisticated taste of real French dishes at those prices. Another thing that I really enjoyed was that I could meet new people there. Since the restaurant is very small, customers stand close to each other. This makes it easy to talk to other customers. We met a group of people who were at a table next to us. They happened to go to the same university as us. They are majoring in English. Two of them are members of *Ochiken*. I'm sure you know them. Talk to you soon.

Best regards,
Jack

(213 words)

1. Has Saki been to a *tachinomi* restaurant?

____

2. Which *tachinomi* place did Jack go?

____

3. What kind of food did Jack and his friends eat?

____

4. Who did Jack meet at the restaurant?

____

Write your reply to Jack

上記のメールへの返信を書いてみましょう。

Unit 4 Convenience Store

コンビニ

Reading and Listening 英文を聞いて，空欄を埋めましょう。

14

There are various views on the very first convenience stores in Japan. One [1] ________________ has it that convenience stores first opened in Aichi Prefecture in the 1970s. After that, many convenience stores appeared and began to spread [2] ________________ in the 1990s. At first they weren't open for 24 hours. However, many started to be open all night within a few years after the first convenience stores appeared.

As of March 2018, the [3] ________________ of convenience stores in Japan was more than 56,000. The prefecture that has the most convenience stores is Tokyo, with more than 7,000 stores, followed by Osaka and Aichi. On the other hand, the prefecture that has the fewest convenience stores is Tottori with [4] ________________ than 250 stores, followed by Shimane.

When looking at the number of convenience stores, Seven Eleven, Family Mart and Lawson are the big three. Although Tokyo and the [5] ________________ areas have more Seven Eleven stores than Family Mart or Lawson, there are more Family Mart stores in the Tokai and Kinki areas.

You can buy anything from food and drinks to sundries and some household drugs at convenience stores. You can also pay utility bills, send and receive parcels, and buy [6] ________________ kinds of tickets, such as concert tickets and sporting-event tickets.

(210 words)

True or False

本文の内容と合っている場合は T，合っていない場合は F を選びましょう。

1. The first convenience store opened in Aichi in 1990. T F
2. Shimane has more convenience stores than Tottori. T F
3. You can't pay for electricity and water at a convenience store. T F

Select Words

本文の内容に合うように，空欄に入れる語を a ～ d から選びましょう。

1. The number of convenience stores in Japan (　　　) increased in the 1990s.

   a. slowly　　**b.** sharply　　**c.** gradually　　**d.** finally

2. Osaka has (　　　) convenience stores than Aichi.

   a. most　　**b.** many　　**c.** much　　**d.** more

3. You can not only buy snacks (　　　) also household drugs at a convenience store.

   a. while　　**b.** and　　**c.** but　　**d.** or

Listen, Write and Answer

音声を聞いて質問を書き取り，その質問に答えましょう。 15

1. Q [　　　　　　　　　　　　　　　　　　　　]

   A ______________________________________

2. Q [　　　　　　　　　　　　　　　　　　　　]

   A ______________________________________

3. Q [　　　　　　　　　　　　　　　　　　　　]

   A ______________________________________

4. Q [　　　　　　　　　　　　　　　　　　　　]

   A ______________________________________

Conversation

16

あなた（A）はコンビニでアルバイトをしています。外国人 Jack（B）と話をするという設定で会話文の続きを作成し，パートナーとやり取りをしましょう。

At a convenience store

A: Next person in the line, please.

B: I'll take a pork bun.

A: OK. One *Nikuman*. Is that all?

B: I also want to buy a cup of your fresh coffee.

A: Regular or large?

B: Regular.

A: Here is a cup. Please use the self-service coffee maker.

Continue the Conversation

会話を続けましょう。

B:

A:

B:

A:

B:

A:

Useful Words and Phrases

come to : ～になる ⇒ Your total comes to 500 yen.
form : 用紙 ⇒ Do you have a form for a home delivery service?
fill in : ～を記入する ⇒ Please fill in the form.
heat up : 温まる ⇒ Do you want this to be heated up?
stamp : 切手 ⇒ Do you sell postage stamps?
copy machine : コピー機 ⇒ Where is the copy machine?
queue/line : 列 ⇒ Please wait in the queue.
aisle : 通路 ⇒ You can find it at the end of this aisle.
point card : ポイントカード ⇒ Do you have a point card?
change : おつり ⇒ Here is your change.

Message to a Friend

次の電子メールを読み，下記の質問に答えなさい。

17

Hi Saki,

Do you often go to convenience stores? I've been going to one almost every day since I came to Japan. As the name suggests, convenience stores in Japan are very convenient. I can buy anything. Of course food and drinks, not to mention some health care products and underwear. If you look at food, they have a variety of cup noodles, snacks and bentos. Some products are found only at convenience stores. In fact, there are some products that are sold only at particular convenience stores. There are seasonal products, too. Winter-only chocolates, summer-only noodles, etc. It's fun not only to look around but also to eat and compare products.

Nowadays, many of the staff working at convenience stores are foreigners. They communicate with customers in Japanese. This is one example of globalization in Japan. I don't know how much the job pays. I mean the hourly wage. Do you know? I'm thinking to start a part-time job. Working at a convenience store is one option. I usually finish school around 4:30 p.m. So I can start work from 5:00 p.m. or 5:30 p.m. I don't have classes on Tuesday; therefore, I will be able to work all day. What do you think?

Warm regards,
Jack

(208 words)

1. How often does he go to convenience stores?

2. Does he know how much he can earn while working at a convenience store?

3. What is Jack thinking about doing?

4. Which day doesn't Jack have classes?

Write your reply to Jack

上記のメールへの返信を書いてみましょう。

Unit 5 Japanese Fast Food, Gyudon

日本食ファストフード"牛丼"

Reading and Listening 英文を聞いて，空欄を埋めましょう。

18

Yoshinoya opened its first franchise chain store selling the fast food *gyudon* (beef bowl) in 1973. As of 2018, Yoshinoya had become a multinational fast food chain with the motto of "tasty, cheap and fast," and had about 1,200 *gyudon* restaurants in Japan and more than 800 locations [1] ______________.

Gyudon was first introduced as *gyunabe*. *Gyunabe* wasn't popular because of the tough [2] ______________ and gaminess. In the Meiji era, beef was a symbolic food of a refined civilization and enlightenment. Many *gyunabe* restaurants opened, and it became a popular dish at the time. *Gyunabe* restaurants used to add a miso, bean paste to get [3] ______________ of its gaminess. It wasn't the same as the *gyudon* served these days.

You can find *gyudon* restaurants everywhere in Japan just like convenience stores, and most of them are open 24 hours, so you can eat *gyudon* [4] ______________ you want. They serve not only *gyudon* but also curry and rice, chicken, pork, breakfast specials as well as side dishes. It's no [5] ______________ to say that *gyudon* is, in a sense, one of the national dishes of Japan. Some *gyudon* restaurants install meal-ticket vending machines with information in Chinese, Korean and English to make them more foreigner-friendly. A *gyudon* restaurant is, [6] ______________, a popular choice with foreign tourists.

(213 words)

True or False

本文の内容と合っている場合はT，合っていない場合はFを選びましょう。

1. Yoshinoya has about 2,000 *gyudon* restaurants abroad. T F

2. There were many *gyudon* restaurants in the Meiji era. T F

3. *Gyudon* restaurants serve only a beef-related menu. T F

Select Words

本文の内容に合うように，空欄に入れる語（句）をa～dから選びましょう。

1. *Gyunabe* wasn't popular at first because of the (　　　) of the beef.

   a. looks　**b.** shape　**c.** taste　**d.** price

2. The taste of *gyunabe* in the Meiji era was (　　　) *gyudon* nowadays.

   a. different from　**b.** similar to　**c.** used to　**d.** the same as

3. *Gyudon* restaurants have chicken dishes as (　　　).

   a. good　**b.** many　**c.** much　**d.** well

Listen, Write and Answer

19

音声を聞いて質問を書き取り，その質問に答えましょう。

1. Q [　　　　　　　　　　　　　　　　　　　　]

   A ____

2. Q [　　　　　　　　　　　　　　　　　　　　]

   A ____

3. Q [　　　　　　　　　　　　　　　　　　　　]

   A ____

4. Q [　　　　　　　　　　　　　　　　　　　　]

   A ____

Conversation

20

あなた（A）は牛丼屋の店員です。外国人 Jack（B）は初めて来店しました。会話文の続きを作成し，パートナーとやり取りをしましょう。

At a *gyudon* restaurant

A: いらっしゃいませ！ How many, please.

B: I'm by myself.

A: Help yourself to any seat. What can I get you?

B: One *gyudon*, please.

A: Sure. Which size?

B: Regular, please.

A: OK. How do you like your *gyudon*?

Continue the Conversation

会話を続けましょう。

B:

A:

B:

A:

B:

A:

Useful Words and Phrases

regular size/serving : 並盛 ⇒ One regular size please.
extra-large size/serving : 特盛 ⇒ I want one extra-large size.
extra soup : 汁だく ⇒ One *gyudon* with extra soup.
red pickled ginger : 紅ショウガ ⇒ Please help yourself to red pickled ginger.
extra beef : 頭大盛り ⇒ I want *gyudon* with extra beef.
to go : 持ち帰り ⇒ I want one large size *gyudon* to go.
take-away : 持ち帰り ⇒ One regular size chicken bowl, take-away, please.
sprinkle : ～を振りかける ⇒ You can sprinkle chili peppers on it.
chopsticks : はし ⇒ Do you have chopsticks?
bill : 札 ⇒ I only have 10,000 yen bill.

Message to a Friend

次の電子メールを読み，下記の質問に答えなさい。

21

Hi Saki,

I'm not sure if I told you this before. The first meal I had when I came to Japan was *gyudon*. Since then, I've loved *gyudon*. I like my *gyudon* with extra soup, *tsuyudaku*. I always order a bowl of miso soup with *gyudon*. Some *gyudon* restaurants offer a free miso soup with every order of *gyudon*. It's very nice, isn't it? I also order *oshinko*, pickled vegetables once in a while. There are many *gyudon* restaurants. Each of them has distinctive tastes, a secret recipe, unique features, and different services. It's hard to decide which one is the best.

As you know, *gyudon* restaurants serve not only *gyudon* but also curry and rice, and rice bowls with chicken, with pork, and some other combinations. Nowadays, I sometimes order the chicken. They also serve alcohol and several side dishes to go with beer for *choinomi*, having a few drinks.

I ate *gyudon* three days in a row last week. I went to three different *gyudon* restaurants. I saw quite a few foreigners there. I'm sure the good combination of sweet and salty flavor is suited to the foreigners' palate. Writing about *gyudon* is making me hungry.

Best,
Jack

(200 words)

1. What does Jack always order with *gyudon*?

____

2. Does he have a particular *gyudon* restaurant that he likes the best?

____

3. What does Jack sometimes order at a *gyudon* restaurant these days?

____

4. How many times did Jack eat *gyudon* last week?

____

Write your reply to Jack

上記のメールへの返信を書いてみましょう。

Unit 6 Japanese Spa

スーパー銭湯

Reading and Listening 英文を聞いて，空欄を埋めましょう。

22

Life in the city can 1 ________________ be stressful. Too many people, too much noise, and too many working hours make you uptight. People therefore need to take a 2 ________________ once in a while. One way to get away from stress and relax in Japan is to go to a spa, or super *sento*.

A Japanese spa is like an *onsen*, a hot spring. One difference between Japanese spas and *onsen* is whether the hot water in the bathtub meets the 3 ________________ necessary to be called an *onsen* or not. Some spas have *onsen* ingredients, but others don't. They just use heated tap water. Even though a spa uses only tap water, it still gives people a relaxing feeling when they 4 ________________ themselves in a large, hot bathtub.

At the spa, you will be given a *yukata*, or loungewear, at the reception desk. They usually have several indoor and outdoor bathtubs with different water 5 ________________ , Jacuzzi and saunas. They also offer resting rooms, restaurants, a massage room, and an amusement area. Therefore, after taking a bath, people wear a *yukata* and can relax or take a nap in a resting room. Some spas are open 24 hours, so people can stay overnight. It is usually less expensive 6 ________________ with staying at a hotel.

(212 words)

True or False

本文の内容と合っている場合はT，合っていない場合はFを選びましょう。

1. All spas and *onsen* in Japan are the same. T F
2. An officially certified *onsen* must meet certain requirements. T F
3. You can stay overnight in some spas. T F

Select Words

本文の内容に合うように，空欄に入れる語（句）をa～dから選びましょう。

1. People living in the city have (   ) lives.

   a. comfortable **b.** stressful **c.** different **d.** easy

2. Taking a bath makes you (   ).

   a. have relaxed **b.** relaxed **c.** relaxingly **d.** relaxing

3. Staying at a super *sento* is usually (   ) than staying at a hotel.

   a. less cheap **b.** cheap **c.** cheaper **d.** cheapest

Listen, Write and Answer

音声を聞いて質問を書き取り，その質問に答えましょう。 23

1. Q [   ]

   A ____

2. Q [   ]

   A ____

3. Q [   ]

   A ____

4. Q [   ]

   A ____

Conversation

24

あなた（A）はスパの受付でアルバイトをしています。外国人 Jack（B）は初めて来店しました。会話文の続きを作成し，パートナーとやり取りをしましょう。

At a spa

A: Welcome to Spa Land Seven. Do you have a membership card?

B: No. This is my first time to come here.

A: OK. Let me explain our system.

B: Thank you.

A: First, you can choose how long you want to stay. Here is the list of times.

B: OK. I'd just like to stay for three hours.

A: Three hours. OK, I will give you your yukata. What is your size?

Continue the Conversation

会話を続けましょう。

B:

A:

B:

A:

B:

A:

Useful Words and Phrases

coin : 硬貨 ⇒ Do you have a 100 yen coin?
receipt : 領収書 ⇒ Here is your receipt.
available : 利用できる ⇒ We have three massage chairs available.
take off : ～を脱ぐ ⇒ Please take off your shoes at the entrance.
floor : 階 ⇒ The restaurant is on the second floor.
locker : ロッカー ⇒ You can use a locker to keep your belongings in.
valuables : 貴重品 ⇒ You can leave your valuables at the front desk.
open-air bath : 露天風呂 ⇒ We have two open-air baths.
nap : 昼寝 ⇒ I like to take naps.
bathing suits : 水着 ⇒ No bathing suits may be worn in the bath.

Message to a Friend

次の電子メールを読み，下記の質問に答えなさい。

25

Hi Saki,

I was very busy and tired due to the assignment deadline of my international business class last week. Satoshi, one of my classmates, said to me, "Why don't we go to a super *sento* to relax and refresh?" I knew that a super *sento* was a kind of *onsen* place, but I had never been before. He took me to one where he had been before. We went there at a quarter past 10 in the morning, so it wasn't so crowded. They have a price list according to how long you stay. We decided to stay for three hours. We paid the money and were given a locker key and a *yukata*.

We went to the men's area, took all our clothes off, and that began our *hadaka no tsukiai*. There were all kinds of baths, such as an open-air bath, a bubble bath, a sauna, etc. We spent one hour trying every bath and chatted about random stuff. After that, we went to an area with massage chairs. We tried massage chairs, and we both fell asleep. After waking up, we went to the bath area again and enjoyed bathing once more. I was able to get a good rest and recharge my batteries.

Best wishes,
Jack

(211 words)

1. Why was Jack tired?

____

2. Who is Satoshi?

____

3. What time did they go to the super *sento*?

____

4. How long did they stay at the super *sento*?

____

Write your reply to Jack

上記のメールへの返信を書いてみましょう。

Unit 7 Flour Dishes

粉もの

Reading and Listening 英文を聞いて，空欄を埋めましょう。 26

Japanese like flour dishes, which are called *konamono*. *Kona* literally [1] ________________ flour powder. *Mono* means things. *Konamono* is particularly popular in the Kansai region. Typical *konamono* are *takoyaki* and *okonomiyaki*. *Takoyaki* is a Japanese snack of diced octopus cooked in a ball of batter and then covered with a savory sauce, mayonnaise and dried bonito flakes. *Okonomiyaki* is a Japanese-style pancake [2] ________________ various ingredients, such as seafood, pork and vegetables, which is then covered with a savory sauce. *Okonomiyaki* is crispy on the outside and fluffy on the inside. You can [3] ________________ mayonnaise, red ginger, dried bonito flakes or a dried green seaweed called *aonori*.

Okonomiyaki is popular with foreign tourists. Tourists from China and Korea make up the [4] ________________ of all the foreign tourists in Japan; however, the number of tourists from Malaysia is increasing. Most of them are Muslim who live under the Halal System. The Halal System includes very [5] ________________ rules about what people can eat and drink. Recently, some *okonomiyaki* restaurants have begun offering Halal food without pork, which Islamic law forbids eating. There are also vegetarians and vegans among foreign tourists coming to Japan, so the food-service industry has started to meet and [6] ________________ the needs of various kinds of people with different cultures and customs.

(211 words)

True or False

本文の内容と合っている場合はT，合っていない場合はFを選びましょう。

1. *Konamono* is mainly made of flour. T F
2. *Konamono* is eaten only in Osaka. T F
3. There are no *okonomiyaki* restaurants serving Halal food. T F

Select Words

本文の内容に合うように，空欄に入れる語（句）をa～dから選びましょう。

1. People in the Kansai area (　　　) *konamono*.

   a. rely on　**b.** depend on　**c.** call on　**d.** are keen on

2. Pork and squid are (　　　) ingredients of *okonomiyaki*.

   a. irregular　**b.** standard　**c.** rare　**d.** local

3. Islamic people can be (　　　) food in Japan these days.

   a. satisfied with　**b.** satisfied to　**c.** satisfied from　**d.** satisfied of

Listen, Write and Answer

音声を聞いて質問を書き取り，その質問に答えましょう。 27

1. Q [　　　　　　　　　　　　　　　　　　　　]

   A ____

2. Q [　　　　　　　　　　　　　　　　　　　　]

   A ____

3. Q [　　　　　　　　　　　　　　　　　　　　]

   A ____

4. Q [　　　　　　　　　　　　　　　　　　　　]

   A ____

Conversation

28

あなた（A）はお好み焼き店でアルバイトをしています。外国人 Jack（B）とその友人が来店しました。会話文の続きを作成し，パートナーとやり取りをしましょう。

At an *okonomiyaki* restaurant

A: いらっしゃいませ！ Do you have a reservation?

B: No, we don't.

A: OK. How many in your party?

B: Two.

A: This way, please. Can I get you something to drink?

B: Two draft beers, please.

A: I'll be right back with your drinks.

Continue the Conversation

会話を続けましょう。

B:

A:

B:

A:

B:

A:

Useful Words and Phrases

topping : トッピング ⇒ What kind of toppings would you like?
griddle : 鉄板 ⇒ Watch out! The griddle is very hot.
draft beer : 生ビール ⇒ We serve chilled draft beer.
bottled beer : 瓶ビール ⇒ I prefer bottled beer to draft beer.
tip : チップ（をあげる） ⇒ Tipping isn't necessary.
batter : 生地，衣 ⇒ There is a small piece of octopus inside the ball of batter.
disposable chopsticks : 割りばし ⇒ We need an extra pair of disposable chopsticks.
as (if) you like : お好みで ⇒ You can add mayo as you like.
confirm : ～を確認する ⇒ Let me confirm your order.
chow mein : 焼きそば ⇒ There is chow mein inside.

Message to a Friend

次の電子メールを読み，下記の質問に答えなさい。

29

Hi Saki,

I learned a new Japanese word today. *Konamono*. Do you know the word? A friend of mine, Koki, and I went to an *okonomiyaki* restaurant for lunch today. I had eaten *okonomiyaki* before, but I didn't know the word, *konamono*. I now love *konamono*. It's not only delicious but also fun to prepare.

At the restaurant we went to today, we prepared our own *okonomiyaki* by ourselves. We both ordered *buta tama*, which is *okonomiyaki* with pork. Koki was good at cooking the *okonomiyaki*. I did pretty well, too, but unfortunately I wasn't successful at turning it over. Although it didn't have a beautiful moon-like shape, the taste was really good. I like my *okonomiyaki* extra crispy on the outside, so I cooked it well. I'm not a mayo lover, so I only spread the savory sauce over it. My toppings were red-pickled ginger, *aonori* and bonito flakes. When adding bonito flakes on hot *okonomiyaki*, the flakes move around as if they are alive. We also ordered beer. *Okonomiyaki* goes very well with icy cold beer. We had one too many!

Do you know *monjayaki*? Koki explained it to me, but I couldn't quite understand what it was. I will order it and try it the next time.

All the best,
Jack

(214 words)

1. What did Jack order at an *okonomiyaki* restaurant?

2. Does he like mayonnaise?

3. How does he describe the bonito flakes on *okonomiyaki*?

4. What did they order with their *okonomiyaki*?

Write your reply to Jack 上記のメールへの返信を書いてみましょう。

Unit 8 Karaoke

カラオケ

Reading and Listening 英文を聞いて，空欄を埋めましょう。 30

Japanese people like to sing. Some people sing to reduce stress, while others sing just for fun. Karaoke is one entertainment outlet of Japanese 1 ________________ culture. Karaoke is defined as a type of entertainment in which people sing popular songs while recorded music is played. The word "karaoke" has become established as an English word.

Karaoke was 2 ________________ in the 1960s in Japan. When karaoke became a trend, people usually enjoyed it at bars or pubs. Later on, karaoke boxes appeared and became popular. People go to karaoke boxes with friends, colleagues or even 3 ________________. A karaoke box is a place with multiple rooms containing karaoke equipment. A large room for a big group who want to go on a singing binge, a mid-sized room for a small group of 4 ________________ friends or a singles party, a small room for a couple on a date, and a very small room for one person who just wants to practice singing. People rent rooms by the 5 ________________. Many karaoke boxes are open 24 hours a day and serve food and drinks.

Looking at the current situation of karaoke abroad, there are many karaoke places in Asian countries 6 ________________ Singapore and Thailand; however, karaoke isn't that popular in Western cultures.

(207 words)

True or False

本文の内容と合っている場合はT，合っていない場合はFを選びましょう。

1. Karaoke originated in Japan. T F
2. People can order food and drinks at a karaoke box. T F
3. Karaoke is very popular all over the world. T F

Select Words

本文の内容に合うように，空欄に入れる語（句）をa～dから選びましょう。

1. Karaoke (   ) in the 1960s.

   a. introduced **b.** was introduced **c.** introduces **d.** has introduced

2. Karaoke boxes have (   ) kinds of rooms.

   a. any **b.** various **c.** few **d.** much

3. Karaoke is popular in Asian countries (   ) in European countries.

   a. but also **b.** not so **c.** but not **d.** not even

Listen, Write and Answer

音声を聞いて質問を書き取り，その質問に答えましょう。 31

1. Q [   ]

   A ____

2. Q [   ]

   A ____

3. Q [   ]

   A ____

4. Q [   ]

   A ____

Conversation

32

あなた（A）はカラオケ店でアルバイトをしています。そこに外国人 Jack（B）とその友人（C）が来店しました。店内での会話文の続きを作成し，パートナーとやり取りをしましょう。

At a karaoke box

A: Welcome to Nice Karaoke. Are you a member? If not, may I please see your ID?

C: Yes, I am a member. Here is my membership card.

A: Which type of karaoke do you prefer? J or D?

B: What are the differences?

A: J has more songs than D. Also, both have a scoring function, but D's scoring function is more accurate than J's.

B: Which do you like?

C: Let's choose D then.

Continue the Conversation

会話を続けましょう。

A:

B:

A:

B:

A:

B:

Useful Words and Phrases

book : 予約する ⇒ Your room is booked for one hour.
minimum : 最低 ⇒ The minimum drinking age is 20.
require : ～を必要とする ⇒ This restaurant requires men to wear a jacket and tie.
coupon : クーポン ⇒ This coupon gives you one hour free.
all-you-can-eat : 食べ放題 ⇒ All-you-can-eat for 1,500 yen.
fill out : ～を記入する ⇒ Please fill this out.
ID : 身分証明書 ⇒ Can I see your ID?
intercom : インターフォン ⇒ Please use the intercom to order drinks.
remote : リモコン ⇒ Please pass me the remote.
extend : ～を延長する ⇒ We would like to extend the karaoke session.

Message to a Friend

33

次の電子メールを読み，下記の質問に答えなさい。

Hi Saki,

How are things going? I know that you study so hard. I'm sure you'll be able to pass the selection examination for a good overseas program. I'm crossing my fingers for you. I'm also preparing an application for a research grant within my department. There are so many pages in the grant application. The passing rate is approximately 50%. I'll do my best, so please wish me luck.

Yesterday, I went to karaoke for a change. Takao came along with me. Takao has a membership at Nice Karaoke. It usually costs 400 yen per hour per room with free drinks between 12 p.m. to 6 p.m., but it's only 300 yen with a membership. We booked the room for three hours and split the bill. They allow customers to bring their own food.

I practiced some Japanese songs, and he practiced English songs. I like Southern All Stars. I sang some of their songs. Takao watched the movie "Bohemian Rhapsody" the other day, so he wanted to sing some of Queen's songs. We chose "We Are the Champions" and "We Will Rock You" and sang them like crazy. We really had a great time together. Maybe you should come with us the next time to refresh yourself.

Take care,
Jack

(212 words)

1. How much did they pay for drinks?

____

2. Why did they get a discount?

____

3. How much did each person pay?

____

4. Can customers provide their own food?

____

Write your reply to Jack

上記のメールへの返信を書いてみましょう。

Unit 9 Seating Charges at Japanese Restaurants

お通し

Reading and Listening 英文を聞いて，空欄を埋めましょう。

34

Tourists who [1] ________________ at a typical *izakaya* are often surprised about a special fee added on to their bill. In fact, some of them complain to staff about this extra charge being tacked on to the bill. This charge is not found abroad, so it is a bit puzzling for foreigners [2] ________________ in Japan. In Japanese it is called *otoshi,* but it has been translated in English as a seating charge, a cover charge or even as a compulsory appetizer. This custom has been carried out since years back [3] ________________ some customers would sit at a table for hours, ordering just a small bit of food and drink, and taking over the table depriving the owner of making sufficient money. The *otoshi* consists of a very small dish of food along with the first drink order. The fee for this *otoshi* [4] ________________ from restaurant to restaurant, but on average is about 500 yen.

Some *izakayas* have recently stopped serving *otoshi* or have started explaining about the *otoshi* system in [5] ________________ to avoid problems with foreign tourists who don't know about the custom. In some areas such as Shibuya and Shinjuku, tourist associations issue and sell meal vouchers that include everything from drinks to meals. With these, *izakayas* don't need to be [6] ________________ about any misunderstanding with foreign customers.

(218 words)

True or False

本文の内容と合っている場合はT，合っていない場合はFを選びましょう。

1. All tourists know about the seating charge applied in Japan. T F
2. The charge for *otoshi* is voluntary. T F
3. The custom of *otoshi* started from many years ago. T F

Select Words

本文の内容に合うように，空欄に入れる語をa～dから選びましょう。

1. The (　　　) tourist did not know he had to pay a seating charge.

   a. sensitive　**b.** surprised　**c.** secretive　**d.** selective

2. The word *otoshi* can be (　　　) into English.

   a. taken　**b.** tracked　**c.** translated　**d.** trusted

3. The money for seating (　　　) from restaurant to restaurant.

   a. exchanges　**b.** trades　**c.** varies　**d.** develops

Listen, Write and Answer

音声を聞いて質問を書き取り，その質問に答えましょう。 35

1. Q [　　　　　　　　　　　　　　　　　　　　]

   A ____

2. Q [　　　　　　　　　　　　　　　　　　　　]

   A ____

3. Q [　　　　　　　　　　　　　　　　　　　　]

   A ____

4. Q [　　　　　　　　　　　　　　　　　　　　]

   A ____

Conversation

36

あなた（A）は居酒屋でアルバイトをしています。そこに外国人 Jack（B）とその友人（C）が来店しました。会話文の続きを作成し，パートナーとやり取りをしましょう。

At an *izakaya*

A: Here you are. Beer and today's *otoshi*.

C: I didn't order this. What is this?

B: Oh, this is called *otoshi*. It comes with your drink.

C: Is it free?

A: No, sorry. It's 480 yen.

B: Didn't you know about that?

A: I'm sorry, but it is a kind of Japanese custom at many pubs and restaurants in Japan.

Continue the Conversation

会話を続けましょう。

C:

A:

B:

C:

B:

C:

Useful Words and Phrases

shift : シフト ⇒ I will the work night shift tomorrow.
complain : 不満を言う ⇒ Some people complain about everything.
tack on : ～を上乗せする ⇒ The shop tacks on an additional 15% as a service fee.
bill : 請求書 ⇒ I received a bill for 3,000 yen.
upscale : 高級な ⇒ Recently, many upscale restaurants have been opened here.
deprive : ～を取り上げる ⇒ He deprived his child of toys.
atmosphere : 雰囲気 ⇒ I like the atmosphere of the restaurant.
dine out : 外食する ⇒ I don't often dine out.
all in all : 全体として ⇒ All in all, the food was good at the restaurant.
another round : おかわり ⇒ Would you like another round?

Message to a Friend

次の電子メールを読み，下記の質問に答えなさい。

37

Hi Saki,

Last night I went to an *izakaya* with a friend visiting Japan from New York. He loved the atmosphere of the place, but he was somewhat surprised about a small dish of food given to us soon after we sat down. The waitress called it *otoshi*. It came quickly as soon as we were seated along with our draft beer. My friend asked me if I had ordered this small dish of food. I told him I did not and that this was the way many small Japanese restaurants began the meal. He wanted to know if I was ever angry that I was given something I did not order. I explained it was part of the culture of Japanese dining out and it was relatively cheap at a charge of roughly 500 yen. I explained to my friend that at times the small *otoshi* dish was a kind of nice surprise.

Since my friend was really hungry, he thought the *otoshi* was a way to eat a bit, drink a bit, and then wait for the ordered items to be brought to the table. It was an interesting custom that he can tell all about when he returns home.

Keep in touch,
Jack

(206 words)

1. Where is Jack's friend from?

____

2. What was he surprised about at the *izakaya*?

____

3. What did they order for drinks?

____

4. Did he eventually accept the idea of the *otoshi*?

____

Write your reply to Jack

上記のメールへの返信を書いてみましょう。

Unit 10 Second-Hand Store

リサイクルショップ

Reading and Listening 英文を聞いて，空欄を埋めましょう。 38

Things can be [1] ________________ anywhere in the world, but buying something new in Japan can easily empty your wallet. Moving into an apartment in Japan is a big money [2] ________________ with several different deposits needed, a fee to a realtor and other unique fees. After paying out all that money, you then must begin to furnish the apartment, which is also a really big drain on your savings.

A second-hand store can help you save [3] ________________ a bit by buying some used goods. You can see a variety of second-hand stores all over the city, and the larger ones sell an amazing selection from furniture to electronic goods and everything in between. All products at stores are thoroughly cleaned, fixed if needed and then sold at [4] ________________ prices. Buying something used and refraining from buying something new helps the recycling movement. Also, the item another no longer needs just might turn out to be your [5] ________________ found treasure!

Some second-hand stores are open 24 hours a day. Whenever you have time and don't have anything to do, a second-hand store is a good place to visit and kill time. You can enjoy just [6] ________________ for recycled clothing, appliances, furniture and other items.

(202 words)

True or False

本文の内容と合っている場合は T，合っていない場合は F を選びましょう。

1. People in Japan only need to pay their monthly rent when moving into an apartment. T F
2. A second-hand store sells only limited kinds of items. T F
3. There are some second-hand stores that are open all night. T F

Select Words

本文の内容に合うように，空欄に入れる語を a ～ d から選びましょう。

1. I looked through all the (   ) in the second-hand store.

   a. seats **b.** bottles **c.** clerks **d.** aisles

2. The (   ) of used items is quite good in Japan.

   a. sum **b.** condition **c.** decision **d.** direction

3. It is often a great waste to throw (   ) something you no longer need.

   a. in **b.** over **c.** out **d.** up

Listen, Write and Answer

音声を聞いて質問を書き取り，その質問に答えましょう。 39

1. Q [   ]

   A ____

2. Q [   ]

   A ____

3. Q [   ]

   A ____

4. Q [   ]

   A ____

Conversation

40

あなた（B）はリサイクルショップでアルバイトをしています。そこに外国人 Jack（A）が来店しました。会話文の続きを作成し，パートナーとやり取りをしましょう。

At a second-hand shop

A: Excuse me.

B: Yes. How may I help you?

A: I’d like to get a washing machine. Where do you keep them?

B: They’re at the end of this aisle ahead. I can take you there.

A: Thank you. Can I ask you some questions about these washing machines?

B: Sure.

A: Thank you.

Continue the Conversation

会話を続けましょう。

B:

A:

B:

A:

B:

A:

Useful Words and Phrases

shipping cost : 送料 ⇒ That price includes the shipping cost.
handling fee : 手数料 ⇒ You have to pay 500 yen for the handling fee.
distribution : 流通 ⇒ The company has a good distribution system.
listed price : 定価 ⇒ Customers don’t usually pay the listed price.
discount price : 割引価格 ⇒ He ordered the book at a discount price.
up-to-date : 最新 ⇒ This book is up-to-date.
sum : 合計 ⇒ The sum is 80 yen short.
assess : ～を査定する ⇒ My used stereo was assessed at a price much higher than I expected.
aisle : 通路 ⇒ You can find the book at the end of the aisle.
shelf : 棚 ⇒ There are many books on the shelves.

Message to a Friend

次の電子メールを読み，下記の質問に答えなさい。

41

Hi Saki,

I have just moved into a new apartment. Moving to a new place in Japan is incredibly expensive in the very beginning. I just keep paying all kinds of fees and deposits, not to mention the expensive rent. I am nearly broke.

I did, however, find a way to cut down on expenditures by using a second-hand store for purchasing some items. I bought a kitchen table with two chairs and a washing machine at a second-hand store. It did not cost me a lot. This second-hand store has an amazing selection of used electronic goods, musical instruments, furniture and even Japanese antiques.

Browsing at a second-hand store can be an interesting experience. It is a special feature in Japan that when someone sells something to a second-hand store, it usually is in really excellent condition. The table with chairs and the washing machine that I bought were almost like new, but I paid much less for them than I would have paid if brand new. People who bring their unwanted goods are paid a relatively small sum from the second-hand store, but it is much better to recycle your unusable goods in this manner than just simply throwing out what could be of use to others.

BR,
Jack

(211 words)

1. Why is Jack nearly broke?

____

2. Where did he go to buy things more cheaply for his new apartment?

____

3. What did Jack buy for his new apartment?

____

4. What is generally the condition of items sold at a second-hand store?

____

Write your reply to Jack

上記のメールへの返信を書いてみましょう。

Unit 11 Kawaii Culture

かわいい文化

Reading and Listening 英文を聞いて，空欄を埋めましょう。 42

Kawaii is the Japanese word for "cuteness" and an international 1 ________________. *Hello Kitty* and other commercialized characters have spread far beyond Japan. Youngsters are finding kawaii idols on Instagram and following them as fans.

Kawaii consists of big, puppy-eyed cartoon anime, the Japanese term for "animation," characters and 2 ________________ pastel or brightly colored fashion. Some youngsters dress as their favorite characters from anime featuring futuristic heroes in action-led stories as well as from cartoons, video games and comic books. Dressing up as a character first began in New York in 1939 and then grew 3 ________________ among anime fans in Asia. But it was not known as cosplay until 1983, when it was mentioned in Japanese magazines. Japan hosted the first ever World Cosplay Summit in 2003, and a championship was 4 ________________ in 2005. Cosplaying makes people feel special. They like creating costumes and being someone else. They can be a different person in their costumes. Also, it's a great way to make new friends.

5 ________________ days, in keeping with the worldwide popularity, many kawaii exhibitions in Japan are accommodating non-Japanese fans. Many of the displays are trilingual, with Japanese, English and Chinese translations. Even if foreign tourists don't know Japanese, they can 6 ________________ read the descriptions.

(206 words)

True or False

本文の内容と合っている場合はT，合っていない場合はFを選びましょう。

1. Youngsters play video games to be kawaii. T F
2. The first cosplay summit was held in New York. T F
3. Cosplaying helps people to make friends. T F

Select Words

本文の内容に合うように，空欄に入れる語をa～dから選びましょう。

1. *Hello Kitty* has been ( ) all around the world.

   a. expected **b.** exported **c.** influenced **d.** imported

2. Some youngsters ( ) their favorite animation characters' fashion.

   a. play **b.** sell **c.** imitate **d.** protect

3. Descriptions of displays at many kawaii exhibitions are written ( ) English.

   a. in **b.** by **c.** for **d.** of

Listen, Write and Answer

音声を聞いて質問を書き取り，その質問に答えましょう。 43

1. Q [ ]

   A ______________________________

2. Q [ ]

   A ______________________________

3. Q [ ]

   A ______________________________

4. Q [ ]

   A ______________________________

Conversation

44

あなた（A）は雑貨店でアルバイトをしています。そこに外国人 Jack（B）が来店しました。会話文の続きを作成し，パートナーとやり取りをしましょう。

At a *Kawaii* variety store

A: Hi, can I help you?

B: Yes, thank you. Does this T-shirt come in pink?

A: No, sorry, just purple. Are you looking for a gift?

B: Yes. I'm looking for something for my friend's daughter.

A: How old is she?

Continue the Conversation

会話を続けましょう。

B:

A:

B:

B:

B:

A:

Useful Words and Phrases

come in : ～を入手できる，売られる ⇒ Does this sweater come in blue?
go well with : ～に似合う，ちょうど良い ⇒ This dish goes well with red wine.
try on : ～を試着する ⇒ May I try this on?
Thanks anyway. : (いずれにしても，とにかく) ありがとう。
feel free to : ご自由に (お気軽に) ～ください ⇒ Feel free to ask me any questions.
fitting room : 試着室 ⇒ Where is the fitting room?
looks good on you : あなたに似合う ⇒ This jacket looks good on you.
be into : ～に夢中，はまっている ⇒ I'm into American comics these days.
stock : 在庫 ⇒ I'm sorry, but that item is out of stock.
refund : 返金 ⇒ I would like to have a refund for the T-shirt I bought.

Message to a Friend

次の電子メールを読み，下記の質問に答えなさい。

45

Hi Saki,

I had wanted to see real kawaii stores in Japan, and finally one of my friends took me to Kiddy Land yesterday. Can you believe that they have six floors and two basement levels full of different toys of so many cartoon characters? It was the greatest selection of kawaii brands I've ever seen. I wandered around for an hour. Before I knew it, I had a basketful of interesting things I could not buy in my country. I bought many souvenirs for my relatives. I was not sure what to buy for my teacher's daughter, so I asked one of the workers. She recommended "Sailor Moon" goods. "Sailor Moon" was a 1990s manga and a gateway into anime for many Western children. Some kawaii girls in Sailor Moon fought to save the universe! I got a T-shirt with Sailor Jupiter for her.

The store is usually very crowded, but we were lucky to be able to go there on a weekday. Every display and all the walls were filled with kawaii toys. I hear that this store is decorated according to the seasons, so each visit means something different. Let's go there again next winter to see Christmas decorations!

Best,
Jack

(204 words)

1. Where did Jack go with his friends yesterday?

____

2. How many floors are there in Kiddy Land?

____

3. What did Jack buy for his teacher's child?

____

4. When will Jack and Saki visit this store again?

____

Write your reply to Jack

上記のメールへの返信を書いてみましょう。

Unit 12 Soba

そば

Reading and Listening 英文を聞いて，空欄を埋めましょう。 46

Soba is a noodle made from [1] ________________ flour. It is a long, thin noodle and is usually brown in color because of the color of buckwheat. *Soba* noodles can be served quickly and are inexpensive, tasty, and above all, nutritious. Many people, particularly office workers, prefer to order *soba* for lunch. Most companies allow their [2] ________________ only an hour at noon for lunch. Thus, workers have to have a quick lunch at nearby restaurants.

Soba has quite a long history. It is said that buckwheat, the main ingredient of *soba*, was introduced from China to Japan. Because buckwheat could grow in [3] ________________ weather conditions as well as in a short period of time as compared with rice, the [4] ________________ of buckwheat was carried out more than 1,000 years ago. In the Edo period, *soba* noodles were eaten in nearly the same manner as they are today.

From the more than 20,000 restaurants serving *soba* noodles nowadays, we can tell how popular they are in Japan. [5] ________________ to one's taste, *soba* noodles can be eaten in two different ways. One is where *soba* noodles are eaten hot, being served in hot broth. The other way is where the noodles are chilled in cold water and eaten cold, being [6] ________________ in a sauce. (211 words)

True or False

本文の内容と合っている場合は T，合っていない場合は F を選びましょう。

1. *Soba* noodles are cheap, but nutritious. T F
2. Buckwheat can grow only in mild weather. T F
3. Japanese people don't eat their *soba* cold. T F

Select Words

本文の内容に合うように，空欄に入れる語（句）を a ～ d から選びましょう。

1. Most companies (　　　) their workers only an hour at noon for lunch.

   a. give　　**b.** make　　**c.** stay　　**d.** take

2. It is said that buckwheat (　　　) from China to Japan.

   a. was flown　　**b.** was changed　　**c.** was brought　　**d.** was replaced

3. In the Edo period, *soba* noodles were eaten (　　　) in the same manner as they are today.

   a. completely　　**b.** always　　**c.** never　　**d.** almost

Listen, Write and Answer

音声を聞いて質問を書き取り，その質問に答えましょう。 47

1. Q [　　　　　　　　　　　　　　　　　　　　]

   A ____

2. Q [　　　　　　　　　　　　　　　　　　　　]

   A ____

3. Q [　　　　　　　　　　　　　　　　　　　　]

   A ____

4. Q [　　　　　　　　　　　　　　　　　　　　]

   A ____

Conversation

48

あなた（A）はそば店でアルバイトをしています。そこに外国人 Jack（B）とその友人たちが来店しました。注文をとる会話の続きを作成し，パートナーとやり取りしましょう。

At a soba restaurant

A: Hi. How are you? Take any seat you like.

B: OK. We'll have a seat by the window, then.

A: Here are your *oshibori* and a menu.

B: Thank you.

A: Would you like to order now?

B: Yes, We'll have some cold *soba*. Let me see ... *tenzaru* and two *mori-soba*, please.

A: Yes, one *tenzaru* and two *mori-soba*. Anything else?

Continue the Conversation

会話を続けましょう。

B:

A:

B:

A:

B:

A:

Useful Words and Phrases

broth : だし汁 ⇒ Some people like *soba* served in hot broth.
slurp :（音をたてて）食べる ⇒ When you eat *soba*, it is all right to slurp it.
buckwheat flour : そば粉 ⇒ *Soba* noodles are made from buckwheat flour.
wheat flour : 小麦粉 ⇒ *Udon* noodles are made from wheat flour.
second helping : おかわり ⇒ Would you like a second helping?
especially : 特に ⇒ *Soba* noodles are popular, especially for lunch.
condiment : 薬味 ⇒ Japanese horseradish, *wasabi*, is often used as a condiment.
Japanese horseradish : わさび ⇒ Japanese horseradish stings in your nose.
deep-fried tofu : 油揚げ ⇒ *Kitsune soba* has deep-fried tofu on top of it.
let me see : ええと～ ⇒ Let me see, what shall I order?

Message to a Friend

49

次の電子メールを読み，下記の質問に答えなさい。

Hi Saki,

How have you been? It's been almost three months since we last met. Time passes so quickly, doesn't it? Is everything going well at college? How is your summer term going? Are you taking two classes again this summer? As for me, I'm taking two classes so that I can hopefully graduate at the end of the fall semester.

By the way, do you remember that new building being built near my apartment? The construction was completed last month, and a *soba* restaurant called "Edoya" has opened on the first floor. Many customers have lined up during lunchtime since it opened.

As you know, my favorite food is *soba*. I can eat *soba* eight days a week! So I went there the other day with my classmates, Ken and Tadashi. I had a type of *soba* called *ebi-tenzaru* because I like my *soba* cold on a hot summer day. Well, it was very tasty and much better than I expected. Ken and Tadashi liked the *soba*, too. I also came to like the place. It was a cozy little restaurant with a sense of a traditional Japanese atmosphere. I must take you and your brother to the restaurant sometime. I will write you again soon.

With regards,
Jack

(210 words)

1. When did he last meet Saki?

2. With whom did he go to the restaurant?

3. What kind of *soba* did he order?

4. What else did he like besides the *soba* he ordered?

Write your reply to Jack

上記のメールへの返信を書いてみましょう。

Unit 13 Bento

弁当

Reading and Listening 英文を聞いて，空欄を埋めましょう。

50

When it comes to eating lunch, many people in Japan think of a bento, or a boxed lunch. Students bring a [1] ________________ bento to school, and many workers bring a bento box to work so they can enjoy their favorite bento at the office.

Making a bento is not just putting rice and [2] ________________ into a bento container; it is an act of expressing one's fond feelings to those who will receive it. Mothers get up early in the morning, think long and hard, and finally decide what should be prepared for the day's bento for their children.

Bentos have been around for quite some time. People as far back as the Edo period enjoyed eating a bento on such [3] ________________ as flower viewings, tea parties and Kabuki plays. The bento has now become a central part of Japanese culture.

Not all bento lunches are made at home. There are a wide [4] ________________ of bento boxes sold at convenience stores and department stores. Bento boxes sold at major train stations or on express trains all over Japan are called *ekiben*. *Ekiben* are usually [5] ________________ with some local specialties that make them popular with commuters and travelers. Ordinary bento boxes and *ekiben* are [6] ________________, priced at around five hundred to one thousand yen.

(212 words)

True or False

本文の内容と合っている場合はT，合っていない場合はFを選びましょう。

1. Very few workers enjoy eating a boxed lunch at their workplace. T F

2. Making a boxed lunch can sometimes require a good amount of thinking. T F

3. Bentos have become so popular that we can now buy them at shops such as convenience stores and department stores. T F

Select Words

本文の内容に合うように，空欄に入れる語（句）をa～dから選びましょう。

1. Making a bento is not (　　　) putting rice and ingredients into a bento container.

   a. usually　　b. always　　c. also　　d. simply

2. You can buy (　　　) bento boxes at convenience stores.

   a. a large variety of　　b. a limited number of
   c. very few types of　　d. only a few kinds of

3. You can purchase bento boxes at (　　　) prices.

   a. surprising　　b. outrageous　　c. reasonable　　d. unbelievable

Listen, Write and Answer

音声を聞いて質問を書き取り，その質問に答えましょう。 51

1. Q [　　　　　　　　　　　　　　　　　　　　　　　　]

   A ____

2. Q [　　　　　　　　　　　　　　　　　　　　　　　　]

   A ____

3. Q [　　　　　　　　　　　　　　　　　　　　　　　　]

   A ____

4. Q [　　　　　　　　　　　　　　　　　　　　　　　　]

   A ____

Conversation

52

あなた（A）は弁当屋でアルバイトをしています。そこに外国人 Jack（B）が来店しました。会話の続きを作成し，パートナーとやり取りしましょう。

At a bento store

A: Good day. How can I help you?

B: Hi. I'd like to buy a bento.

A: Which bento would you like?

B: What is today's special?

A: A bento with fried chicken, spinach namul and seasoned rice.

B: Well, I'll take it then, and a bottle of cold Japanese green tea.

A: Sure. That will be 648 yen, including tax, please.

Continue the Conversation

会話を続けましょう。

B:

A:

B:

A:

B:

Useful Words and Phrases

a boxed lunch : 弁当 ⇒ Boxed lunches are popular among students.
ingredient : 材料 ⇒ What ingredients did you use in this curry and rice?
recipe : レシピ，料理法 ⇒ Jane taught me this recipe.
home-made : 手料理の ⇒ I miss home-made meals.
express :（気持ちを）表す ⇒ I can't even begin to express my gratitude.
one's feelings : 感情 ⇒ It is a way of expressing one's feelings.
local specialty : 地方の名物 ⇒ What is a local specialty of Sendai?
affordable : 手ごろな ⇒ A cup of coffee is being sold at an affordable price.
on the shelf : 棚の上 ⇒ There are many bento boxes on the shelf.
next to : ～の隣に ⇒ I sat down next to my teacher.

Message to a Friend

次の電子メールを読み，下記の質問に答えなさい。

53

Hi Jack,

What are you up to lately? Are you still going to the *Igo* school after class? I've no idea of how to play *Igo* myself, but I guess you must be doing a lot of thinking and analyzing different tactics. Thank you for your kind e-mail last Sunday. Yes, winter is just around the corner, and the cold winter weather will come again soon in our town, too.

I am now learning to cook and can make a bento to take to school. I am fed up with the same old menu at the cafeteria, and the foods they serve are far from cheap for a school cafeteria. I'm not making any fancy bento like the one a mother makes for her child with sausages cut into the shape of an octopus or anything like that. My bento recipes require just a few simple ingredients. I can use leftovers, vegetables, and for example, use any fish from the fridge. No special skills for the cutting board are needed. By making a bento, I become more concerned with the foods I eat. Anyway, my own lunch is super delicious and nutritious, and above all, it costs less than the cafeteria. I'll make one for you sometime.

Your friend,
Saki

(210 words)

1. Where is Jack likely to go after class?

____

2. Which season can you infer from the e-mail?

____

3. Are the foods in the cafeteria cheap?

____

4. Does Saki have special cooking skills?

____

Write your reply to Saki

上記のメールへの返信を書いてみましょう。

Unit 14 Shrine
神社

Reading and Listening 英文を聞いて，空欄を埋めましょう。

54

Jinja are Shinto shrines, where Shinto deities are enshrined. Shinto is the 1 ________________ religion of Japan, and it has been around in the country since ancient times. Many Japanese may visit a shrine on different occasions. They will pay a visit to a shrine to make wishes on New Year's Day, to 2 ________________ the birth of a child, to pray for the healthy growth of children on the occasion called "Shichi-go-san" and so on.

When visiting a shrine, you will come to at least one *torii*. A *torii* is a 3 ________________ Japanese gate that stands at the 4 ________________ of a shrine. You should make one polite bow at the *torii* to show respect to the deity of the shrine. As you proceed to the hall of worship, be careful not to walk in the center of the path since it is 5 ________________ to be the walkway used by the deity.

Before reaching the hall of worship, there is a place called *temizuya* where you should stop to wash your hands and rinse out your mouth to 6 ________________ yourself. Finally, at the hall of worship, where you make wishes to the deity, bow twice and clap your hands twice, and pray. Then make one more deep bow to end your prayer.

(210 words)

True or False

本文の内容と合っている場合は T，合っていない場合は F を選びましょう。

1. Shinto is a religion that originated in a country outside of Japan. T F
2. There are some shrines which do not have a *torii*. T F
3. It is good manners to wash one's hands before making wishes. T F

Select Words

本文の内容に合うように，空欄に入れる語（句）を a ～ d から選びましょう。

1. Shinto has been (　　　) in Japan since ancient times.

   a. written　**b.** practiced　**c.** encouraged　**d.** abandoned

2. Visitors should walk (　　　) the path as they approach a shrine.

   a. in the middle of　**b.** in front of　**c.** on either side of　**d.** in the back of

3. *Temizuya* is a place where visitors (　　　).

   a. take a rest　**b.** make wishes　**c.** drink water　**d.** purify themselves

Listen, Write and Answer

音声を聞いて質問を書き取り，その質問に答えましょう。

55

1. Q [　　　　　　　　　　　　　　　　]

   A ______________________________

2. Q [　　　　　　　　　　　　　　　　]

   A ______________________________

3. Q [　　　　　　　　　　　　　　　　]

   A ______________________________

4. Q [　　　　　　　　　　　　　　　　]

   A ______________________________

Conversation

56

あなた（A）は正月，神社でアルバイトをしています。そこに外国人 Jack（B）がやってきました。神社での買い物について Jack に説明をします。会話の続きを作成し，パートナーとやり取りしましょう。

At a shrine

A: Happy New Year!

B: The same to you.

A: How may I help you, sir?

B: Well, what do you have here? What are these for?

A: These are charms for good health, and those are for safe driving. Would you like one?

B: Yes, I would like to have two charms for good health. One for my girlfriend, and one for me.

A: Here they are. 1,400 yen, please.

Continue the Conversation

会話を続けましょう。

B:

A:

B:

A:

B:

A:

Useful Words and Phrases

deity : 神 ⇒ Let's pray to the deity.

indigenous :（その土地に）固有の ⇒ The Maori are the indigenous people of New Zealand.

religion : 宗教 ⇒ Shinto is the indigenous religion of Japan.

bow : お辞儀する ⇒ He bowed to show his respect to his teacher.

clap :（手を）たたく ⇒ Clap your hands twice.

purify : ～を浄化する ⇒ Purify yourself by washing your hands.

ancient times : 古代 ⇒ The ceremony dates back to ancient times.

make a wish : 願いごとをする ⇒ I made a wish at the shrine.

worship : 礼拝 ⇒ Proceed to the hall of worship.

Message to a Friend

57

次の電子メールを読み，下記の質問に答えなさい。

Hi Jack,

How are you getting along on the first day of the year? I wish you a joyful and prosperous new year. Thank you for all your help and kindness last year. I've really enjoyed knowing and studying with you since last spring.

Have you eaten *Osechi-ryori*, traditional Japanese New Year's foods? They are made from ingredients thought to bring fortune and health. Shrimps, black beans and herring roe are some typical *Osechi* ingredients. Shrimp represents longevity because the shape of the shrimp looks like an old man with a bent back, whereas black beans represent hard work because the color of the beans symbolizes the darkened suntan of workers.

You mentioned that you were going to visit Meiji Jingu Shrine during the New Year's holidays. I suggest that you avoid visiting the shrine during the first three days of the New Year because hundreds of thousands of people will come to visit. You won't have enough time to enjoy the shrine.

When you go there, remember to stop at the *temizuya*, where you can purify yourself by washing your hands and rinsing out your mouth. Also, don't forget to bring some small coins. People customarily throw coins into an offertory box when they make wishes at the hall of worship.

With regards,
Saki

(215 words)

1. What month of the year can you infer from the e-mail?

2. What do you call the traditional food eaten during the New Year's holidays?

3. When will Jack probably visit the shrine to avoid the huge crowds?

4. What do people customarily do when they make wishes at a shrine?

Write your reply to Saki

上記のメールへの返信を書いてみましょう。

Unit 15 Onsen

温泉

Reading and Listening 英文を聞いて，空欄を埋めましょう。

58

Japan is one of the most 1__________________ countries in the world, with more than 100 volcanoes. Many of these volcanoes produce *onsen*, or hot springs. According to the Ministry of 2__________________ in 2015, there are more than 3,000 *onsen* resorts across Japan. As you can tell from this great number of *onsen* resorts, many Japanese like *onsen* to a greater or lesser degree, and *onsen* have long been a part of Japanese 3__________________. Some of the reasons why Japanese like *onsen* may have something to do with the climate of Japan. Although the climate differs from region to region, Japan has four clear-cut seasons in most parts of the country, with summers being not only hot, but also 4__________________ and muggy, and winters being very cold. These natural conditions make Japanese people love 5__________________ in an *onsen*.

One of the oldest *onsen* in Japan is Dogo Onsen in Matsuyama, Ehime Prefecture. It is said to have existed for 3,000 years, and over its long history, a countless number of people have enjoyed visiting and bathing there. It is also said that *onsen* have various 6__________________ qualities. They seem to possess properties for healing wounds, aches and pains.

(197 words)

True or False

本文の内容と合っている場合は T，合っていない場合は F を選びましょう。

1. There are very few volcanos in Japan. T F

2. People in Japan love to visit an *onsen* in part due to the four distinct seasons. T F

3. It is said that minerals in hot springs are good for health. T F

Select Words

本文の内容に合うように，空欄に入れる語（句）を a ～ d から選びましょう。

1. Many Japanese ( ) *onsen.*

   a. dislike **b.** are fond of **c.** never visit **d.** are uninterested in

2. The climate ( ) from region to region in Japan.

   a. moves **b.** stays **c.** changes **d.** increases

3. It is said that Dogo Onsen has ( ) for more than 3,000 years.

   a. existed **b.** disappeared **c.** exploded **d.** sunk

Listen, Write and Answer

音声を聞いて質問を書き取り，その質問に答えましょう。 59

1. Q [ ]

   A ______________________________

2. Q [ ]

   A ______________________________

3. Q [ ]

   A ______________________________

4. Q [ ]

   A ______________________________

Conversation

60

あなた（A）は温泉ホテルでアルバイトをしています。そこに外国人 Jack（B）がやってきました。温泉の利用の仕方について Jack にアドバイスをします。会話の続きを作成し，パートナーとやり取りしましょう。

At a hotel by the ocean

A: Welcome to the Ocean View Hotel. Have you been to our hotel before?

B: No, this is the first time. We've heard that you have a very nice outdoor hot spring with a great ocean view.

A: Yes, all our guests enjoy soaking in the *rotenburo*.

B: Could you give us any tips as to how we use it?

A: Sure. Two things you need to remember. First, wash your body before getting into the bath. Second, be sure not to put your towel in the bath.

B: All right, we'll remember that. Well, I can't wait to take the bath.

A: Enjoy our *rotenburo*. Just sit back and relax.

Continue the Conversation

会話を続けましょう。

B:

A:

B:

A:

B:

Useful Words and Phrases

ocean view：海の見える ⇒ I had a room with an ocean view.
hot spring：温泉 ⇒ There are thousands of hot springs in Japan.
outdoor hot spring：露天風呂 ⇒ The hotel is equipped with an outdoor hot spring.
public bath：公衆浴場 ⇒ There used to be many public baths in Japan.
soak in：〜につかる ⇒ We are soaking in a hot bath.
fatigue：疲労 ⇒ I was suffering from fatigue.
get into：〜に入る ⇒ He is working hard to get into Harvard University.
humid：湿気のある ⇒ The climate here is humid.
environment：環境 ⇒ Eco-cars are environment friendly.
region：地域 ⇒ The climate differs from region to region.

Message to a Friend

次の電子メールを読み，下記の質問に答えなさい。

61

Hello Saki,

How is life treating you lately? Just as planned, I'm going to graduate at the end of this semester. Time flies! I haven't decided yet whether I will go straight on to graduate school or get a job first to save up money for my future study.

By the way, my cousin Steve and two other guys from my class and I are taking a graduation trip to Takayama and Gero Onsen in Gifu Prefecture after taking the final exams in February. We need a chance to recuperate from our senior year. This will be my second visit to an *onsen* in Japan. Both places are not too far from where I reside and commute to college in Nagoya.

Takayama is a little over a two-hour drive from Nagoya. It is an old town which flourished in the Edo period and keeps its old town atmosphere. If only we had a car. There is nothing like a road trip along beautiful mountainous regions for a change of scenery. But this time, we are going to take a bus. Gero Onsen, located conveniently between Nagoya and Takayama, is rated one of the most famous hot-spring resorts in Japan. We're really looking forward to the trip.

With regards,
Jack

(209 words)

1. What year is Jack finishing up at his college?

____

2. Is Jack visiting an *onsen* for the first time?

____

3. Where is Jack's college located?

____

4. Does Jack have his own car to drive to Takayama?

____

Write your reply to Jack

上記のメールへの返信を書いてみましょう。

Glances of Japan [B-898]

日本文化とおもてなし英語

第1刷 2020年 4月 1日
第3刷 2023年 3月 31日

著 者 坂部 俊行 Toshiyuki Sakabe
岡島 徳昭 Noriaki Okajima
ターノフ・ハワード Howard Tarnoff

発行者 南雲一範 Kazunori Nagumo
発行所 株式会社 南雲堂
〒162-0801 東京都新宿区山吹町361
NAN'UN-DO Publishing Co., Ltd.
361 Yamabuki-cho, Shinjuku-ku, Tokyo 162-0801, Japan
振替口座：00160-0-46863
TEL: 03-3268-2311（営業部：学校関係）
03-3268-2384（営業部：書店関係）
03-3268-2387（編集部）
FAX: 03-3269-2486

編集者 伊藤宏実
組版・印刷 啓文堂
装 丁 NONdesign
検 印 省 略
コード ISBN978-4-523-17898-9 C0082

Printed in Japan

落丁・乱丁，その他不良品がございましたら，お取り替えいたします。

E-mail nanundo@post.email.ne.jp
URL https://www.nanun-do.co.jp/